THE LAST BYZANTINE

AND OTHER POINTED POEMS

THE LAST BYZANTINE

AND OTHER POINTED POEMS

J.R. CAMPANELLI

LEONINE PUBLISHERS
Phoenix, Arizona

The Scripture citations used in this work are taken from *The Holy Bible*, Revised Standard Version, Second Catholic Edition, copyright © 2006, by Ignatius Press.

Published by Leonine Publishers LLC
Phoenix, Arizona
USA

Cover image, "Constantine XI Palaiologos, the Last Byzantine Emperor," by Unknown. Licensed under Public Domain via Commons, https://commons.wikimedia.org/wiki/File:Constantine_XI_Palaiologos_miniature.jpg#/media.

ISBN-13: 978-1-942190-18-9

Library of Congress Control Number: 2015953830

Printed in the United States of America

10 9 8 7 6 5 4 3 2 1

Visit us online at www.leoninepublishers.com
For more information: info@leoninepublishers.com

Dedicated to my wife
On our 25th anniversary

CONTENTS

PART I

Would that you were hot …

PART II
Would that you were cold ...

PART III
Turn and become like children ...

PREFACE

Christianity is under siege. In the Middle East, Asia, and Africa the systematic use of military force and terror against the Church and its adherents is aimed at extirpating the Faith from its ancient soil. In the West, the tactics are more subtle, but directed to a similar end. The growing progressive faction of modern society is determined to embark on the greatest social experiment since Constantine the Great promulgated the Edict of Milan some seventeen centuries ago: the repudiation of Christian morality as the foundation of our very culture. And when they have succeeded in hacking off the branch upon which we are all perched, they expect not the withering decay of detritus but the unencumbered flowering of a post-Christian utopia.

The poems in this collection represent my own musings. These are on the centrifugal forces that have led us to this watershed moment in the history of our great Faith and the civilization it has engendered and sustained for so many centuries.

The collection is divided into three parts. In the first, *Would that you were hot...*, the poems reflect a time when Christianity was the undisputed cornerstone of western civilization. In the title poem, which recounts the siege and fall of Constantinople to the Ottoman Turks, only the common bond of Christianity was capable of overcoming the disparate cultural, commercial and imperial interests of the Greek and Italian residents to forge a desperate defense of the "pearl of Christendom." The other poems reflect the role of faith in many aspects of life: struggle, pain, gratitude, praise, and above all, hope.

In the second part, *Would that you were cold…*, the poems reflect a burgeoning cynicism and rejection of absolute truth. Even amid the growing agnosticism, however, truth cannot be buried, but remains discoverable to all people open to receiving the gift of Christ's love.

In the final section, *Turn and become like children…*, the voice of the innocent cries out against hollow relativism, and rises to seek meaning amid the rubble of a post-Christian wasteland. When the future seems bleakest, it will be the next generation that reclaims its inheritance and renews Holy Mother Church. To them goes the task of restoring her to her rightful place in the hearts and minds of men and women in the joyful anticipation of the return of our Savior!

J.R. Campanelli
Greenville, South Carolina
The Feast of the Assumption
Anno Domini 2015

PART I

Would that you were hot …

CONSTANTINOPLE
DURING THE SIEGE OF 1453

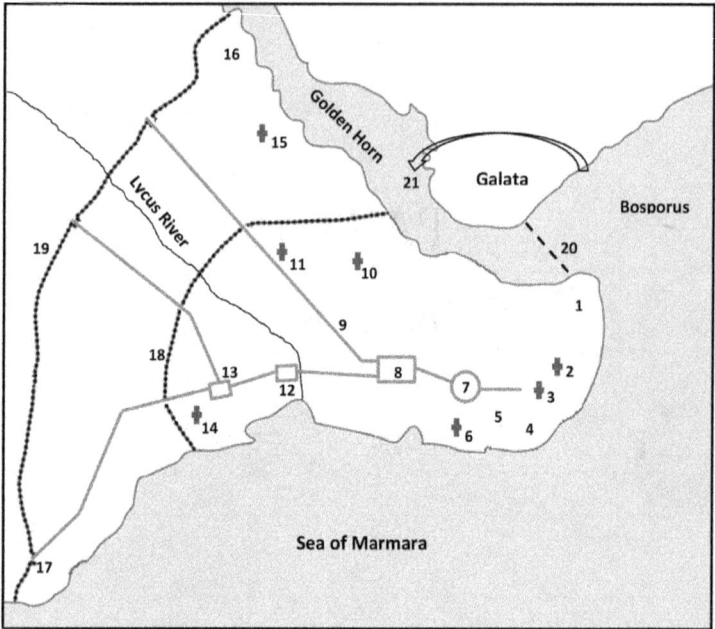

1. Acropolis
2. St. Irene
3. St. Sophia (*Hagia Sophia*)
4. Great Palace
5. Hippodrome
6. Sts. Sergius and Bacchus
7. Forum of Constantine
8. Forum of Theodosius
9. *Mese*
10. Christ *Pantocrator*
11. The Holy Apostles
12. Forum *Bovis*
13. *Forum of Arcadius*
14. *Theotokos Panachrantos*
15. *Theotokos Pammakaristos*
16. Blachernae Palace
17. Golden Gate
18. Walls of Constantine
19. Walls of Theodosius
20. Harbor chain
21. Overland route from the Bosporus to the Golden Horn

THE LAST BYZANTINE

Who'll hear the tale of Constantine,
Constantinople's liege?
Sovereign of the Byzantines
Through mighty Mehmet's siege.

What bitter fate, O Constantine,
Has raised you to your throne
To face grave perils yet unseen
By emperors of East Rome?

No solace from Heraclius,
Justinian or Basil,
Whose armies marched victorious,
Whose standards made men tremble.

They gaze on you with sightless eyes
Perched proud in palace halls.
The glory of their empire lies
Behind your city's walls;

Enclosing now Venetians,
With Greeks and Genoese.
Can you defend your kingdom
Amid their uneasy peace?

The Christian princes waver –
Do they not see your woes?
Abandoned like your Savior
And delivered to His foes.

Brave men still fight at your command
So raise the harbor chain;
Take up your sword into your hand
One ally, hope, remains!

Behold the Turkish armada
As it unhindered, floats
Across the placid Marmara
To disgorge its dreaded hosts.

Hear now the Sultan's cannons
Spew forth their hellish loads
At walls that a millennium
Withstood the barbarous hordes.

By day the ceaseless barrage
Of pounding cannon balls;
By night repair the damage
And strengthen crumbling walls.

There is no longer time for rest,
The people need their king!
Your Lord has put you to the test,
Will you His praises sing?

Process with holy icons,
In silent vigil pray.
Cry out *Kyrie Eléison,*
And fight on day by day.

The Turks are great in number.
They thirst for slaves and gold.
But your soldiers spurn their slumber,
And the battered land-walls hold.

Can your empire yet be saved?
Will glory crown your reign?
Many dangers have you braved,
But many more remain.

Galata plays a double game
Across the Golden Horn,
Pledging allegiance to your name
But offering little more.

The Podestà dares not relate
To you the Sultan's plan
To link the harbor to the strait
By road through his own land;

Until your unbelieving eyes
Behold a wondrous thing –
And watch the Turkish galleys rise
From Bosporan moorings.

Conveyed on iron wheels
O'er the hilltop they are borne;
Then, gently, cradled keels
Dip into the Golden Horn.

And now the last safe harbor,
O Constantine, is gone.
And can the final hour
Now be delayed for long?

Besieged by land,
Besieged by sea,
Alone you stand,
So let it be.

Your people trust in piety
As faith tempers their fears,
In their God-protected city
That has stood a thousand years!

Why has the Virgin's icon grown
Too heavy now to bear?
As thunderstorms bring hailstones down
To scatter those in prayer.

And does the suffocating cloud,
From sea to Golden Gate,
Extending like a burial shroud
Foretell the city's fate?

What signifies th'unearthly glow
Atop Justinian's dome?
Some say God's Holy Spirit knows
To leave His ancient home.

Amid these portents gather
The Italian and the Greek,
As reconciled brothers
And together God entreat.

And now the cannon's silence,
The breath before the plunge,
The stealth of slithering serpents
That coil before they lunge.

Stillness permeating the night,
Belies the trials ahead.
Think not upon your city's plight,
Banish all sense of dread.

Gallop 'round the walls once more,
Accept your captains' cheers.
Counsels of escape ignore,
Your cause must triumph here.

Hearken now the trumpet's blast
Before the break of dawn!
The hour of judgment comes at last
In the darkness of the morn.

The soldiers of the crescent moon
Advance to die and kill.
The pearl of Christendom will soon
Be theirs, by Allah's will.

Flanked by loyal Varangians
To the weakest ramparts ride,
And repel on each occasion
The relentless Turkish tide.

But one by one your captains fall.
When brave Giustiniani
Is carried, wounded, from the wall
It emboldens th'enemy.

And with the rising of the orb
The Lycus wall is breached.
And through an unlocked sally door
A palace tower is reached.

The circuit pierced cannot be held.
With transfixed heart you see
The fearsome Janissaries spread
Along the broad Mese.

Can you hear now, Constantine,
Your people's desperate cry?
Amid the pillage and rapine
They suffer and they die.

Saint Sophia holds no safety
As the infidels burst in,
Disrupting sacred liturgy
And slaughtering at whim.

The priests with consecrated hosts
Through stone walls disappear.
The Father, Son and Holy Ghost
Are no longer welcome here.

The tombs of saints and emperors
Cannot protect their dead,
As relics spurned by conquerors
Are tossed to dogs instead.

Holy icons – blest Theotokos –
Are hacked and thrown aground,
While cheers of the victorious
From Blachernae resound.

The sun has risen on a day
Few thought could ever be.
Byzantium falls twenty-ninth May,
Fourteen fifty-three.

What now, unhappy Constantine?
Your destiny is sealed:
Last sovereign of the Byzantines.
Will you to Mehmet yield?

Cast off imperial armor
And plunge into the fray!
Your life but not your honor
You sacrifice this day.

Shed not a tear for Constantine,
His war is past and gone.
The sovereign of the Byzantines
His blessed rest has won.

He fought with noble valor
In the dark shadow of doom.
The words of his sweet Savior
Have led him to the tomb.

I've come to bring a sword, said He,
Not peace to man on earth.
Take up your cross and follow me.
The emperor showed his worth.

THE FATHER OF LIES TRILOGY

You are of your father the devil, and your will is to do your father's desires. He was a murderer from the beginning, and has nothing to do with the truth, because there is no truth in him. When he lies, he speaks according to his own nature, for he is a liar and the father of lies.

John 8:44

SONNETS IN THE TRILOGY

The Sower of Weeds
The Tempter in the Desert
The Bearer of Light

THE SOWER OF WEEDS

The Son of Man my kingdom rent in rising
  from the dead!
And every day I lose more souls as His good
  news is spread.
But I knew man before the Fall, and still I
  know him best.
His path is eas'ly led astray – his heart oft fails
  the test!

Sweet mercy and compassion are a master's
  right to give
To men who sacrifice themselves, not I that
  they should live.
The slaves I seek embrace my creed, wage war
  without respite
For earthly power and the hope of posthumous
  delight.

"Will you, Great One, appear on earth to rule
   now as her lord?"
A messenger I have chosen to wield my
   vengeful sword.
Behold a shoot sprung up from seed sown in a
   barren land;
Reveal to him what he must heed – what he
   must understand.

"Who shall I say commands him to proclaim
   all he has heard?"
Profess the name of He-That-Is and thus
   confound His Word!

THE TEMPTER IN THE DESERT

The gates of hell have not prevailed; the city on
  a hill
These fifteen centuries has stood, and stands to
  mock me still!
The light inside shone brightly – now diffused
  through men of sin.
The walls that weathered blows may be eroded
  from within.

I quoted Scriptures long ago to tempt the
  spotless Lamb.
These words with power to save, perhaps, can
  also serve to damn.
Sola scriptura – raise the cry! Therein each man
  will find
His own truth and thus shall we sever branches
  from the vine.

"This stratagem must fail, Great One, these
    men preach unity.
From fruits of endless schism they will surely
    know our tree."
You credit not enough their pride, the ways of
    saints long dead
Will be ignored as men exalt their meager wits
    instead.

So let us find a haughty monk to raise our cry
    with might,
And man becomes a prism to refract the perfect
    Light!

The Bearer of Light

The cursed lamp of truth He lit two thousand
   years ago,
Through violent storms and darkest night
   persists; remains aglow!
Man's pride provides the bushel for the lamp to
   be obscured
By branding truth ephemeral, uncoupled from
   the Word.

Ennoble pride – cry tolerance! No right, no
   wrong, mere choice!
And the narrow road will broaden as mankind
   heeds my voice.
For as of old, man longs to be a god unto
   himself,
Trusting unfettered reason; truth will languish
   on the shelf.

"But, Great One, surely reason must finally
   yield to Light?
In this, your darkened kingdom, it suffuses
   endless night."
The Light of truth glows brightly, pride's flame
   ignites another:
The light I bear, love of self, eclipsing love of
   brother.

God or devil, saint or sinner – distinctions fade
   away.
My light from Light shall lead them to my
   realm – where night holds sway!

Whispers along the Path

And he said, "Go forth, and stand upon the
mount before the Lord…"

And a great and strong wind tore the
mountains … but the Lord was not in the
wind;

And after the wind an earthquake, but the
Lord was not in the earthquake;

And after the earthquake a fire, but the Lord
was not in the fire;

And after the fire a still small voice.

1 Kings 19:11-12

The wind …

The withering winds of conflict blow;
The foe lies helpless at my feet.
My will and skill exalted
In the wake of his defeat.

I mouth a prayer of thanks to You,
So clearly by my side.
Your grace delivers victory
And sanctifies my pride.

But is it not my brother
Who lies humbled at my feet?
Your voice amid the accolades
Unheard through my conceit.

The earthquake …

Tremors surprise me in the night,
As solid ground melts beneath me.
The world I knew and loved is gone;
My grieving soul left empty.

I raise an angry cry to You,
Demanding You explain!
The life I built, You sanctioned –
And now it seems in vain.

But are Your thoughts so like my own
That I might understand?
In grief and pain I shun Your voice,
And fail to know Your plan.

The fire …

The flames of passion burn within,
And drive me on, relentless.
The fuel is pleasure, fame, and gold;
My appetites are boundless.

I bless You for Creation –
By right mine to enjoy.
To feed the fire becomes an end,
What means I must employ.

But though the flames may now abate
Will they not roar again?
Your voice alone delivers me
To peace without an end.

The still small voice …

You speak to me in whispers,
Persistent, unimpeded
By tremors, flames and gales of life –
But oftentimes unheeded:

Through actions of a stranger,
Or the comfort of a friend,
Coincidences and accidents,
Some hard to comprehend.

Lord, grant me grace to hear You
Whispering in my soul.
Guide me on throughout my life,
And bring me to You whole.

How Grim Indeed

How grim indeed this world of men
Were Jesus never born;
The unredeemed thus condemned
To night without the morn.

The wheat, unharvested, decays.
No rock on which to build.
The prophecies of ancient days
Forever unfulfilled.

Abandoned by uncaring God,
Fallow the virgin womb.
The cross a sign of death raised proud;
Life ending at the tomb.

No shining city on the slope
To pierce the gloom and give men hope.

HERE THEN MY GETHSEMANE

Here then in my Gethsemane,
No garden as of old.
This sterile room my agony
And supplications hold.

No toga'd procurator sits
To sentence me to death;
Replaced by white-robed specialists
Conferring under breath.

No prayer allays th'uncertainty.
Dare I hope to be saved?
Vain plea of all humanity
That judgment be delayed.

And should this day the cup slip past,
Grim Golgotha awaits at last.

THE MOVING FINGER

Some say that time's a cunning thief,
Relentless foe of man.
The angels have eternity,
We've sorrow, toil and pain.

In time man finds redemption,
For angels there is none.
Satan's fall is eternal,
His hubris carved in stone.

In this world of trial and tragedy,
We often fail, it's true;
But time moves on and thus may we
Arise again anew.

So thank we now our sovereign God
For the grace that makes it so:
Though we may fall a thousand times
To hell we need not go.

TO LILITH

O haughty woman who deigns to wed
And disparages the marriage bed;
What pleas can stay God's awful hand
From one so cruel to her own husband?

Far better had you not been born
Than unrepentant judgment morn
Face Him who did of old decree
That out of two one flesh should be;
And mock with proud, unblinking eye
God's own command to multiply.

As Christ is groom, His Church the bride,
For her fecundity He died;
So you the bride, and for your groom
A sterile love and sterile womb –
A stricken wasteland, worn and numb,
That suffers not the children come!

Heed not the brooding prince of hell,
In fallow loneliness to dwell.
There is hope upon the Stygian shore;
Trust in love and live once more!

Daily Blessings

Bless me on Sunday and help me hear
Your voice in the Scriptures that we hold so dear.

Bless me on Monday and help me do
The things in my day that will glorify You.

Bless me on Tuesday and help me see
The beauty Your love has created for me.

Bless me on Wednesday and help me taste
Your generous bounty to share without waste.

Bless me on Thursday and help me feel
The pain of my brothers and sisters to heal.

Bless me on Friday and help me know
Your Spirit will guide me wherever I go.

Bless me on Saturday that I become
Perfect as You are through Jesus, Your Son.

A Gladiator's Prayer

Morituri te salutant, Deus.
Into Your hands my spirit I commend.
Do not forsake Your servant, Lord,
But sheath, I pray, Your righteous sword,
And greet with mercy this unworthy friend.

PART II

Would that you were cold …

The Bread of Life

What use is my life,
The pain, toil and strife?

When all that I have can be plucked away
                … and dust becomes dust …

In squalor of night, or in pallor of day
                … for just and unjust …

To whom shall I go, what words can help stay
                … there's no one to trust …

The growing despair that shuts out the way
                … indulge every lust …

Of life?

L'ÉGLISE DU PARC

There is a vacant church which stands
Across the Parc Terrebonne.
On Sunday walks I climb its steps
Awash in morning sun.

And watch the white-robed lilies sway,
Bowing low before the breeze;
While songs of black-winged prodigals
Ring out from budding trees.

Proud couples stroll the narrow paths
With children in their tow,
And solitary figures read
Reclining on the knoll.

The squirrels with agitated gait
In wariness advance
To picnic tables longing for
The work of human hands.

Inside the church the muted rays
Through colored panes ingress,
And scintillating particles
In solemn dance process.

The empty wooden pews,
And silent stone-faced walls,
Alone bear witness to the god-man
Hanging on the cross.

His face through agony, serene,
Having uttered one last cry.

Forsaken of man,

Forsaken of God,

Forgotten by all,

He dies.

THE VACANT THRONE

… now that I view the scene in retrospect I see
it as a very gentle and firm deportation, taking
me from the country of the well across the stark
frontier that marks off the land of malady.

Christopher Hitchens[1]

Of all the lands I wished to see
The least of these is Malady.

Amid meadow's dew, forest's shade
And sweet oblivion's peaceful wave
It stretches desolate and bare –
A winding, rock-strewn thoroughfare.

Its taste is bitter alkali,
Assaults the tongue and stings the eye;
Its odor antiseptic balm,
The pungent pledge of sterile calm;
Its sound th'unceasing, voiceless drone
Of dull mechanic monotone;
Its touch a death by increments,
Of cold metallic implements.

There is no king in Malady.
A vacant throne breeds anarchy.
The weary traveler besieged
By foul concoctions – fouler deeds!

Were there a strong hand at the helm,
A lord to pacify this realm,
Then Malady would be no more,
And verdant field meet sandy shore.

The sentiment that suffering
Could be a good and sacred thing
Screams blasphemy against the mind!
If truth, then truth is too sublime.

No there's no king in Malady;
There is no king – there cannot be.

BELLAGIO

The end is coming,
Repent your sins,
The Lord will soon return!
Mend your ways,
Make straight the path,
Or you will surely burn!

What incongruity, thought I,
This prophet from a bygone day
Against the dancing fountains lit.

Around him parts the streaming throng
As if in fear of contagion.

These people have no time, my friend,
To heed your vengeful god.
They seek out varied pleasure domes:
The hotels' topless towers
And cacophonous casinos,
Lascivious reviews
And four-star eateries,
Resplendent shopping malls
And throbbing night clubs,
All manner of diversion to titillate the senses
And assuage the sun-parched soul.

Yes, all these wonders man has raised
From the lone and level sands.
What need have we of your deity
When his might imbues our hands?

Oz

Enchanted monkeys are we all,
Dancing on a string
Forged in time immemorial,
Beholden to nothing.

Impulses and DNA
Have made us
What we are today.

No evil
But disease;
No good
But what we please;

And dreams of courage,
Love and truth
To vex a hollow beast.

This creed, they say,
Has drawn away
The curtain to our beings.

COMBOX

Spare us, credulous mystics,
Your self-righteous oracles:
Ex-nihilo creation,
Ancient prophetic verses,
And a god dead, yet alive!

We have rational physics
Which proclaims no miracles:
A quantum fluctuation
Spawns untold multiverses,
And a cat dead, yet alive.

Schrodinger's Fetus

It is both baby
And products of conception;
Then she makes a choice.

A Pok-ta-Pok-alypse

If today the world should end
Let not your heart be troubled, friend,

But thankful were we screaming torn
From insensate oblivion born

To glean upon this passing earth
What days we can of joy and mirth.

And though the shadows lengthen around,
We'll hear our victory cry resound,

Look back in wonder as we await
Our earthly end and eternal fate.

When twilight touches the temple stone
And the serpent god has fled his throne;

When all our deeds and all our desires
Are naught but a memory,
Naught but an echo faint,
Naught but a tale dimly recalled
As by one who from dreaming awakes;

When all that we've known and all we've held dear
Are naught but a globule,
Naught but a drop,
Naught but a swirling protein dissolved
In the vast cenote encompassing time;

What then of love?

The cruelest lie!
The promise of something real
Snatched from eternity

Destined to die,
As the pools of blood congeal
In the sacred city.

Where then the pity, friend,
If today the world should end?

THE CRUX OF
THE MATTER

O Death, O Death where is thy sting
If Christ did truly rise?
But Death has swallowed everything
If in the tomb He lies.

Love one another is the law
If Christ did truly rise.
But love is crushed in hatred's maw
If in the grave He lies.

Blessed are the humble and meek
If Christ did truly rise.
But might is right and rules the weak
If in the dust He lies.

The last are first and first are last
If Christ did truly rise.
But vanity reigns unsurpassed
If in the ground He lies.

Pray for those who would wish you ill
If Christ did truly rise.
But no one hears and heaven's still
If in the earth He lies.

The gates of hell shall not prevail
If Christ did truly rise.
His Church endures to no avail
If with the worms He lies.

To all preach faith, hope, charity
If Christ did truly rise.
Above all we are pitied if
In sheol He abides.

PART III

Turn and become like children …

Nursery Philosophy

Well, I left fairy tales lying on the floor of the nursery, and I have not found any books so sensible since.

G.K. Chesterton[2]

(Richard reads…)

The universe we observe has precisely the
  properties
We should expect if there is, at bottom,
No design, no purpose, no evil, no good,
Nothing but blind, pitiless indifference.[3]

(The class recites…)

Rock a bye, baby, on the treetop
When the wind blows, the cradle will rock.
When the bough breaks, the cradle will fall,
And down will come baby, cradle and all.

(Deepak reads…)

Every person
Is a god in embryo.
Its only desire
Is to be born.[4]

(The class recites…)

"Oh," said the worm,
"I'm awfully tired of sitting in the trees;
I want to be a butterfly
And chase the bumblebees."

(Lao reads…)

Health is the greatest possession.
Contentment is the greatest treasure.
Confidence is the greatest friend.
Non-being is the greatest joy.[5]

(The class recites…)

Humpty Dumpty sat on a wall.
Humpty Dumpty had a great fall.
All the king's horses and all the king's men
Couldn't put Humpty together again.

(Krishna reads…)

Wilt thou weep?
The end of birth is death;
The end of death is birth:
This is ordained![6]

(The class recites…)

The itsy bitsy spider went up the waterspout,
Down came the rain and washed the spider out.
Out came the sun and dried up all the rain,
And the itsy bitsy spider went up the spout again.

(Siddhartha reads…)

A wise man,
Recognizing that the world is but an illusion,
Does not act as if it were real,
So he escapes suffering.[7]

(The class recites…)

Row, row, row your boat
Gently down the stream.
Merrily, merrily, merrily, merrily,
Life is but a dream.

(Bilal reads…)

Allah is Most Great.
There is none worthy of being worshipped but
    Allah.
Muhammad is the Apostle of Allah.
Come to prayer. Come to success.[8]

(The class recites…)

The cock doth crow
To let you know,
If you be wise
'Tis time to rise.

(Moses reads…)

Hear O Israel:
The Lord our God is one Lord;
And you shall love the Lord your God with all
   your heart,
And with all your soul, and with all your might.[9]

(The class recites…)

Twinkle, twinkle little star,
How I wonder what you are;
Up above the world so high,
Like a diamond in the sky.

(John reads…)

And the Word became flesh
And dwelt among us,
Full of grace and truth;
We have beheld His glory.[10]

(The class recites…)

Mary had a little lamb,
Little lamb, little lamb.
Mary had a little lamb
Its fleece was white as snow.

Civics 101: Matrimonial Devolution

Marriage (noun):
The union of a man and a woman,
In an indissoluble bond,
Vowing to love, honor and cherish each other
  unto death,
Giving themselves unreservedly one to the
  other in order to procreate, and
Raising their children in a nurturing family
  environment.

1857 – *Matrimonial Causes Act* establishes marriage as a contract that can be broken by one or both partners.

Marriage (noun):
The union of a man and a woman,
Vowing to love, honor and cherish each other
  unto death,
Giving themselves unreservedly one to the
  other in order to procreate, and
Raising their children in a nurturing family
  environment.

1969 – California becomes the first state to adopt "no-fault" divorce.

Marriage (noun):
The union of a man and a woman,
Giving themselves unreservedly one to the
  other in order to procreate, and
Raising their children in a nurturing family
  environment.

1970 – Title X legislation makes contraception readily available to all Americans.

Marriage (noun):
The union of a man and a woman,
Raising their children in a nurturing family
  environment.

1987 – For the first time in the United States, over one million babies are born to unwed mothers.

Marriage (noun):
The union of a man and a woman.

2015 – The United States Supreme Court rules that same-sex couples have a constitutional right to marry.

Marriage (noun):
Definition not found.

BLACK AND WHITE

I was walking home one afternoon
On a balmy summer's day,
After cooling off in Johnson's pond,
Whistling on my way.

I saw a swirling cloud of dust
Approaching rapidly:
A midnight black convertible.
The driver stopped by me.

    "Where can I get some gas, young man?"
    He called out with a smile.
"Continue on this road," I said,
"Until you reach Carlisle."

"Forgive me for admiring, sir,
Your car. We have a lack,
With dusty roads and summer heat,
Of sports cars painted black."

    "Why thank you boy, I love my ride –
    She's really quite the sight.
    But what you've said just now is wrong
    My car is surely white!"

There was no grin upon his face,
No glimmer in his eye.
This man was being serious,
So I said in reply:

"Black is black and white is white,
It's clear as night and day.
Black is black and white is white,
No matter what you say!"

"Ah," said he, with wistful smile,
"The certainty of youth!
You'll find as you grow older, son,
There is no simple truth.

"For who are you to judge me wrong?
Where do you get the right
To contradict me when I say
My car is painted white?"

"We learned in science class, good sir,
Just what it means to say
An object's black, an object's white
Or different shades of grey.

"A surface that is painted white
Reflects all frequencies of light;
A surface that is painted black
Absorbs all light – reflects none back.

"So black is black and white is white,
Each word has meaning, sir;
Black is black and white is white,
Why surely you concur?"

"Young man, young man,"
He waved his hand, o so wistfully,
"Science cannot understand
What colors mean to me.

"I love the look of my fine car
Against fields of moonlit snow;
Or how the coalescing mist
Gives her a reddish glow.

"There is no finer view, my boy,
Than the ocean's frothy foam
Blowing swiftly across her hood
When along the coast we roam.

"But that word, *black,* evokes in me
The darkness of the pit;
Of lost souls toiling wearily
In tunnels dimly lit;

"Of soot and grime and heaps of slag
Ejected 'midst the roars
Of hellishly hot furnaces
Digesting vulgar ores!

"Now *white* exudes a purity
Of spirit soaring high;
Of knight mounting his charger
With adventure drawing nigh.

"Listen, boy, and hear me well
For that is how I feel
Whenever I climb into my car
And take hold of the wheel:

"A cavalier upon a quest!
No doubt you'll now concede
It is the noble color, white
That best describes my steed?"

His gaze held mine expectantly,
With unspoken demand.
"Thank you for explaining, sir,
I think I understand.

"Black is black and white is white –
You wish it wasn't so.
But black is black and white is white;
Your car is black, you know."

At this his visage darkened and
I heard the engine whine.
He vanished in a cloud of dust
Speaking of pearls and swine.

Now if these pearls were black or white
I did not hear him say.
I shook the dust off from my feet
And whistled on my way.

The Secret Sister

I have a secret sister;
I wish I knew her name.
I don't know what she looks like
But I love her all the same.

I've never held her hand in mine,
We've never run and played.
I've never crawled into her bed
At night when I'm afraid.

She doesn't live inside our home,
I've found no hidden room.
So maybe she's an astronaut
Orbiting the moon!

Or maybe she's a secret spy
Tracking our enemies!
Or maybe she's a pirate girl
Sailing the seven seas!

My friends call me a liar –
They say my sister's just pretend.
I know that I have one,
I just don't know where she went.

I know because I hear my mom
When she thinks I'm asleep.
I listen at the air vent
And I do not make a peep.

She's talking to my sister!
She tells about my day,
About the things I do in school,
About the games I play.

There's no one in the room with her,
My mom is all alone.
So she must be talking to my sister
On a secret phone.

O how she wishes sis was here
To see me as I grow!
And it makes her sad to think about
The love I'll never know.

And I want to ask my mommy
Where my sister is; instead,
I hear her crying softly
And I tiptoe back to bed.

SUESSIAN SOLIPSISM

I look at you, you look at me.
How can I know just what you see?
Red for you and red for me
Is light of the same frequency.
But is red for me like red for you,
Or does my red look like your blue?
This thought just drives me up the wall,
How do I know you see at all?
All I can know of the world around
Is taste, touch, sight, odor and sound.
What if I'm floating all alone
Inside a universe of one,
With wires attached right to my brain
Creating coffee, kisses, rain?
No flowers, buildings, friends, or wife,
Electric impulses my life,
As I drift on to parts unknown
Inside a universe alone.
If this speculation's true
Why keep writing? So, *adieu!*

Goodnight Moon

Goodnight moon.
Goodnight lady on the moon.
Goodnight lady with the sun for a gown.
Goodnight lady with the stars for a crown.
Goodnight Baby snuggling tenderly.
Goodnight Baby smiling down on me.

The night is dark, the night is deep;
A dragon waits that never sleeps.
The baby Boy will strike its head,
And keep me safe tucked in my bed.

Goodnight moon, my day is done.
I'll greet you with the rising sun.

NOTES

[1]Christopher Hitchens, *Mortality*, Twelve Books, 2012.

[2]G.K. Chesterton, *Orthodoxy*, Moody Publishers, 2009.

[3]Richard Dawkins, *River Out of Eden: A Darwinian View of Life*, Basic Books, 1996.

[4]Deepak Chopra, http://www.chopra.com/node/644, 2013.

[5]Lao Tzu, *The Sayings of Lao Tzu*, Kessinger Publishing, 2010.

[6]Krishna, *Bhagavad Gita*, Edwin Arnold tr., Dover Publications, 1993.

[7]Siddartha Gautama, *Wisdom of the Buddha: The Unabridged Dhammapada*, F. Max Muller (ed), Dover Publications, 2000.

[8]Anonymous, Wikipedia entry for *Adhan*, 2013.

[9]Deuteronomy 6:4-5.

[10]John 1:14.

ABOUT THE AUTHOR

J.R. Campanelli is a cradle Catholic with a fondness for expressing in verse his musings on the changing role of Christianity in Western society. Born and raised in Montreal, Canada, he now lives in South Carolina with his wife, Anita, and their daughters, Sara and Alyssa.

About Leonine Publishers

Leonine Publishers LLC makes fine Catholic literature available to Catholics throughout the English-speaking world. Leonine Publishers offers an innovative "hybrid" approach to book publication that helps authors as well as readers. Please visit our web site at www.leoninepublishers.com to learn more about us. Browse our online bookstore to find more solid Catholic titles to uplift, challenge, and inspire.

Our patron and namesake is Pope Leo XIII, a prudent, yet uncompromising pope during the stormy years at the close of the 19th century. Please join us as we ask his intercession for our family of readers and authors.

Do you have a book inside you? Visit our web site today. Leonine Publishers accepts manuscripts from Catholic authors like you. If your book is selected for publication, you will have an active part in the production process. This book is an example of our growing selection of literature for the busy Catholic reader of the 21st century.

www.leoninepublishers.com

www.ingramcontent.com/pod-product-compliance
Lightning Source LLC
Chambersburg PA
CBHW060534030426
42337CB00021B/4252